Teaching Children to
Pray

Grades 1&2

by Mary J. Davis

These pages may be copied.
Permission is granted to the buyer of this book to reproduce,
duplicate or photocopy student materials in this book for use with
pupils in Sunday school or Bible teaching classes.

Rainbow Publishers

Rainbow Publishers • P.O. Box 261129 • San Diego, CA 92196

www.rainbowpublishers.com

Dedication

To my parents, John and Fern; my mom, Phyllis; and all the
siblings — Norma, John, Ron, Dave, Phil, Barb, Kathy, Margie,
Carol and Tommy. And, to Larry, my husband and best friend
since 1967.

TEACHING CHILDREN TO PRAY FOR GRADES 1 & 2
©2003 by Rainbow Publishers, Seventh Printing
ISBN 1-885358-25-3
Rainbow reorder #36613
church and ministry/ministry resources/children's ministry

Rainbow Publishers
P.O. Box 261129
San Diego, CA 92196
www.rainbowpublishers.com

Illustrator: Joel Ryan
Cover Illustrator: Terry Julien

Printed in the United States of America

Contents

Memory Verse Index

Topical Index

Materials to Gather

These activities are especially designed for first- and second-graders — and they require few materials to complete. Listed below are all of the items you will need to lead the activities as they are designed in this book. However, you may eliminate and add as you desire. Some activities call for more supplies than others, so you may select the activity that best meets your class time and available materials. A reproducible note is included at the bottom of this page to garner assistance in collecting multiple materials. Just duplicate, clip and distribute as needed. Check off the items on the list below as you gather them. If available, provide children's scissors — which are easier for small hands to manipulate. All activities calling for "tape" in the materials lists require the clear type of tape.

- ❑ aluminum foil
- ❑ baby food jars, without lids
- ❑ balloons, helium quality
- ❑ Bibles
- ❑ candy bars, 1½" wide
- ❑ chenille stems
- ❑ clothespins, spring-type
- ❑ construction paper, assorted colors
- ❑ craft sticks
- ❑ crayons
- ❑ cups, 3 oz. plain paper
- ❑ felt, various colors
- ❑ foam meat trays or plates
- ❑ glue
- ❑ glue sticks
- ❑ hole punch
- ❑ magnet bits
- ❑ markers, permanent and non-permanent
- ❑ paint, tempera or acrylic, assorted colors
- ❑ paper clips
- ❑ pens
- ❑ pencils
- ❑ plain paper
- ❑ poster board
- ❑ rice or beans, dry
- ❑ sandwich bags
- ❑ scissors
- ❑ soda cans, pull tabs attached
- ❑ stapler
- ❑ stickers, assorted
- ❑ string
- ❑ tape
- ❑ toothpicks
- ❑ transparencies
- ❑ waxed paper
- ❑ wire clothes hangers
- ❑ yarn, assorted colors and lengths

- -

To Families and Friends of First- and Second-Graders

We are planning many special craft activities for your child. Some of these crafts include regular household items. We would like to ask your help in saving the items checked below for our activities.

- ❑ baby food jars, without lids
- ❑ balloons, helium quality
- ❑ candy bars, 1½" wide
- ❑ chenille stems
- ❑ clothespins, spring-type
- ❑ craft (popsicle) sticks
- ❑ cups, 3 oz. plain paper
- ❑ felt, various colors
- ❑ foam meat trays or plates
- ❑ magnet bits
- ❑ rice or beans, dry
- ❑ sandwich bags
- ❑ soda cans, pull tabs attached
- ❑ toothpicks
- ❑ wire clothes hangers
- ❑ yarn, assorted colors and lengths

Please bring the items on _____ .
Thank you for your help!

Preface

Prayer is our lifeline to God. Without prayer, we falter in our walk with Him and give in to worries, fears and even temptations. The time to begin building a powerful prayer life is in early childhood, for children who learn the power of prayer early will have a special relationship with their Lord.

The activities in this book will help students build that strong prayer life. The 27 projects offer a variety of activities to keep students interested while adding to the building blocks of their faith and prayer life. They have been designed with flexibility to serve as independent lessons or as add-ons to your curriculum. They can also be used in Christian schools or at home as family devotion projects. To make selection of the appropriate activity easier, the projects are grouped in four sections: Prayers for Care, Prayers of Commitment, Prayers of Praise and Prayers of Thanks, allowing the teacher or parent to emphasize topics of prayer. Also, on page four you will find a memory verse index, allowing you to choose an activity that applies to a particular verse your class may be studying, and, on page five, a topical index that will assist you in finding the right activity to reinforce your lesson.

Within each activity, you are provided with everything you need to teach a prayer lesson: memory verse, prayer thought (or theme), suggested prayer, a related lesson idea, materials list, pre-class preparation and step-by-step instructions. Each project includes reproducible patterns or illustrations. All activities have been especially designed to meet the abilities and interests of first- and second-graders while also offering a teacher-friendly concept that is a breeze to prepare and teach — making classtime less hectic and more rewarding for both you and the children.

Since these activities are about prayer, it is important for both the adult to lead in prayer and for the children to be encouraged to pray in class. Soon, your children will look forward to prayer time as they work on these exciting activities. What a wonderful foundation to begin and build upon with your students!

Dad's Handy Holder

PRAYER
Dear God, help me to always show my dad how much I love him. Amen.

MEMORY VERSE
We love because he first loved us. 1 John 4:19

PRAYER THOUGHT
I am glad my dad (or grandpa) cares for me.

ITEMS NEEDED
page 12, duplicated
baby food jars, without lids
crayons
markers
scissors
glue
toothpicks
sandwich bags

PREPARATION

Duplicate page 12.

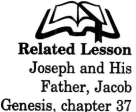

Related Lesson
Joseph and His Father, Jacob
Genesis, chapter 37

DIRECTIONS

1. Focus the class on being thankful for fathers and grandfathers. Be sensitive to those students who do not have a father in the home — perhaps they can give a gift to their grandfather or another adult male.

2. As the children cut out and color the strip from page 12, talk about the blessings God has given us in our families, no matter what type of family we have.

3. After the students have cut out and colored the strip, help them to glue it to the baby food jar.

4. Allow each child to place some toothpicks inside his or her jar for the gift. Say, **When you give this to your dad (or grandpa) tell him that you pray for him and thank God for him.**

5. Give each child a sandwich bag for the Handy Holder to prevent spilling the toothpicks.

6. Close with prayer.

PRAYERS FOR CARE

11

Prayer Finder

PRAYER
God, I will turn to You when I am afraid, tempted to do wrong, worried or lonely. Amen.

MEMORY VERSE
Surely I am with you always. Matthew 28:20

PRAYER THOUGHT
God helps me with my problems.

ITEMS NEEDED
page 14, duplicated
scissors
Bibles
extra plain paper (optional)

PREPARATION
Duplicate page 14.

DIRECTIONS

1. Help the students to look up each of the verses on the Prayer Finder on page 14 and read them aloud. Discuss how each verse helps our needs.

2. Have the students write the Bible verse above the correct reference on the Prayer Finder.

3. Help the students cut out their Prayer Finders on solid lines. Show them how to fold the flaps on the dashed lines toward the center.

4. On the outside of the flaps, instruct the students to write (coordinating verses are in parentheses): 1. Afraid (Heb. 13), 2. Tempted (Heb. 2), 3. Worried (Ps. 55) and 4. Lonely (Matt. 28).

5. Say, **Take your Prayer Finder home with you. When you are afraid, tempted, worried or lonely, look up the verse in your Bible and see what God says.**

6. Pray with the children before they leave the class.

Option: If time allows, have the students trace the shape of their Prayer Finders onto a plain piece of paper. They may look up verses that are meaningful to them and write the verses on their Prayer Finders.

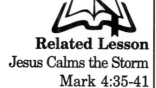

Related Lesson
Jesus Calms the Storm
Mark 4:35-41

PRAYERS FOR CARE

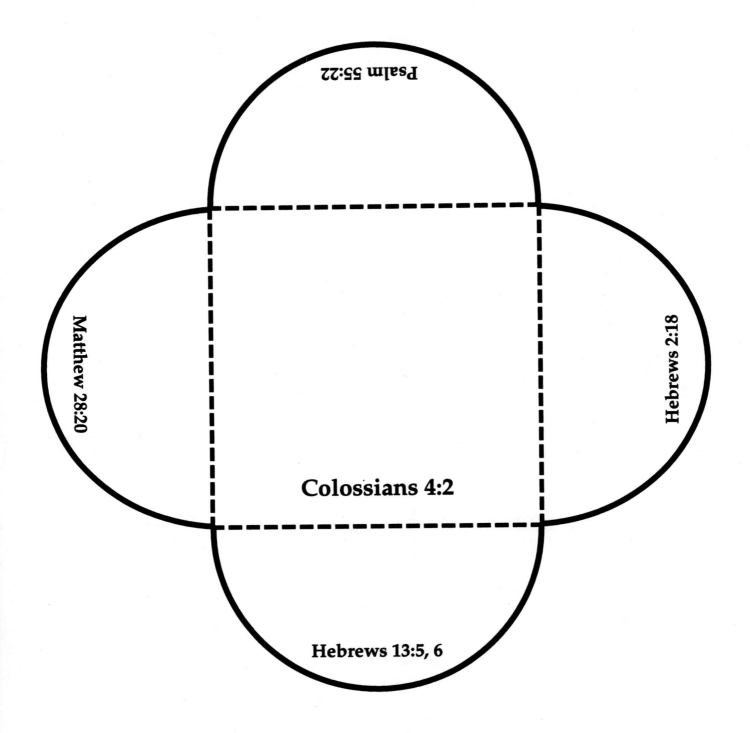

Psalm 55:22

Matthew 28:20

Colossians 4:2

Hebrews 2:18

Hebrews 13:5, 6

14

Care Coupons

PRAYER
Please take care of
my friends. I will
show them Your
love. Amen.

MEMORY VERSE
Pray for each other. James 5:16

PRAYER THOUGHT
I will pray for my friends.

ITEMS NEEDED
page 16, duplicated
scissors
crayons or markers
pencils

PREPARATION

Duplicate page 16. Optional: Make two copies of page 16 for each child.

DIRECTIONS

1. As the students color and cut out the coupons from page 16, talk about praying for each other. Say, **How does it feel to know that someone is praying for you? It makes us feel good, doesn't it? What a special thing, to know that someone is praying for us.**

2. Encourage the students to give their prayer coupons to friends during the following week.

3. If desired, you may provide the students with two copies of page 16 to cut out and color.

4. Close with prayer.

Related Lesson
Peter Escapes
from Prison
Acts 12:1-19

PRAYERS FOR CARE

_____
...is praying for you.

_____
...is praying for you.

_____
...is praying for you.

Jonah Calls for Help

MEMORY VERSE
I called for help, and you listened to my cry. Jonah 2:2

PRAYER THOUGHT
God hears my prayers, wherever I am.

ITEMS NEEDED
page 18, duplicated
crayons or markers
scissors
tape
yarn or string

PREPARATION
Duplicate page 18.

DIRECTIONS

1. Review the story of Jonah as the children color and cut out the fish, the hole in its body and Jonah from page 18. Say, **Do you ever feel that God can't hear your prayers? He can hear us, no matter where we are. He even heard Jonah pray from inside the fish.**

2. Show how to tape a short length of yarn to the back side of the fish so the yarn hangs in the middle of the circle.

3. Have the children tape the picture of Jonah to the other end of the yarn, so he is in the middle of the circle.

4. Close with prayer.

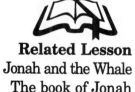

Related Lesson
Jonah and the Whale
The book of Jonah

PRAYERS FOR CARE

Paper Weight Promise

MEMORY VERSE
Come to me, all you who are weary and burdened, and I will give you rest. Matthew 11:28

PRAYER THOUGHT
Jesus will take away our burdens if we trust Him.

ITEMS NEEDED
page 20, duplicated
scissors
crayons or markers
tape
rice, beans or pebbles

Related Lesson
Lilies of the Field
Matthew 6:28-33

PREPARATION
Duplicate page 20. Optional: Make a second copy of page 20 for each student to make as a gift.

DIRECTIONS
1. Make sure the children know what "burdens" and "worries" are. Help them understand that Jesus wants to make the load lighter for us. Say, **Sometimes we worry about things and feel like a heavy load is on our shoulders. Jesus doesn't want us to feel like that. He has promised to take that heavy load and give us rest. Our paper weights will remind us that Jesus wants to give us rest from our burdens.**
2. As the children cut out the box from page 20, guide them so that they will cut only on the solid lines.
3. After they color their boxes, help them to fold inward on the dashed lines to form a box and tape at the seams. Leave the top of the box open.
4. Allow them to fill their boxes about ¼ full with rice, beans or pebbles.
5. Have them tape the top closed. Make sure they place tape along all of the open seams so the filling does not come out of the box.
6. Close with prayer.

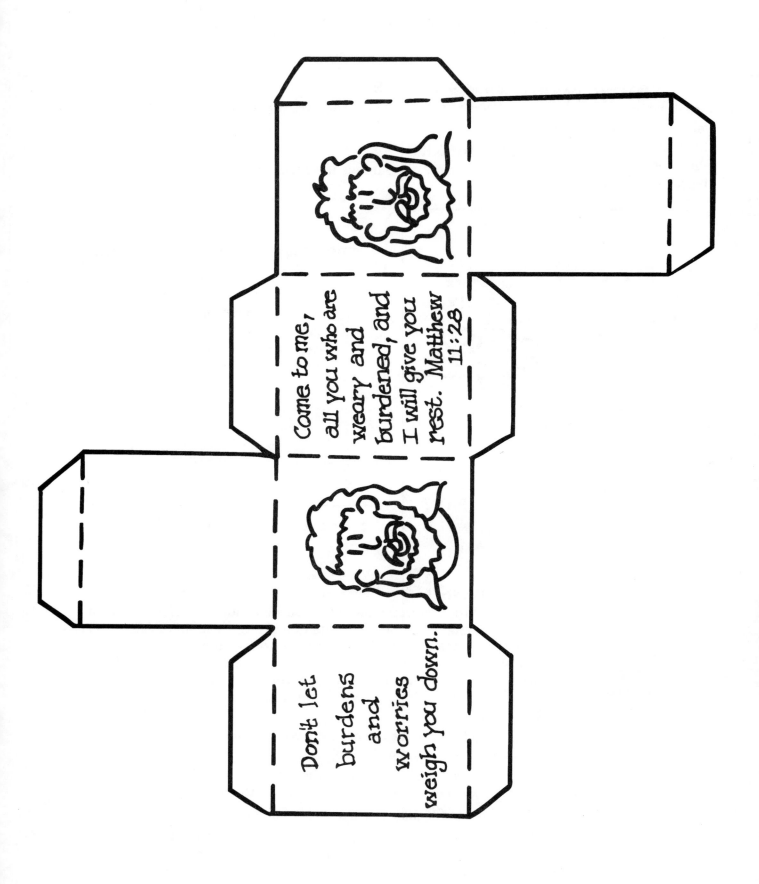

Come to me, all you who are weary and burdened, and I will give you rest. Matthew 11:28

Don't let burdens and worries weigh you down.

Stampin' Love

PRAYER
God, help me to be loving to everyone so others will know that I am Your follower. Amen.

MEMORY VERSE
Love one another. John 13:34

PRAYER THOUGHT
I will show love to everyone.

ITEMS NEEDED
- page 22, duplicated
- foam meat trays or plates
- scissors
- tape
- tempera or acrylic paint, assorted colors
- plain paper
- pencils
- glue
- paint smocks

PREPARATION

Duplicate page 22. If you are using powdered tempera paints, mix them before class time and store in containers with lids. You may want to provide paint smocks (large shirts work well) to protect clothing.

DIRECTIONS

1. Assist the students as they cut out the shapes and the handles from page 22.

2. Show them how to trace the heart patterns onto the foam.

3. Next, the students cut out the foam shapes, then fold the paper handles at the dashed lines and tape them to the backs of the foam shapes.

4. Distribute plain paper and show how to fold it in half to make a card.

5. Pour a thin layer of paint onto a tray or plate. Explain to the students how to dip their foam stamps into the paint and press them onto the card.

6. They may cut out the verses and phrases from the paper patterns and glue them onto the card. Help them write a message on their Valentines.

7. As the students work, help them learn the memory verse. Tell them that a good way to love people is to pray for them.

8. Close with prayer.

Related Lesson
The Greatest Commandment
Matthew 22:34-40

PRAYERS FOR CARE

21

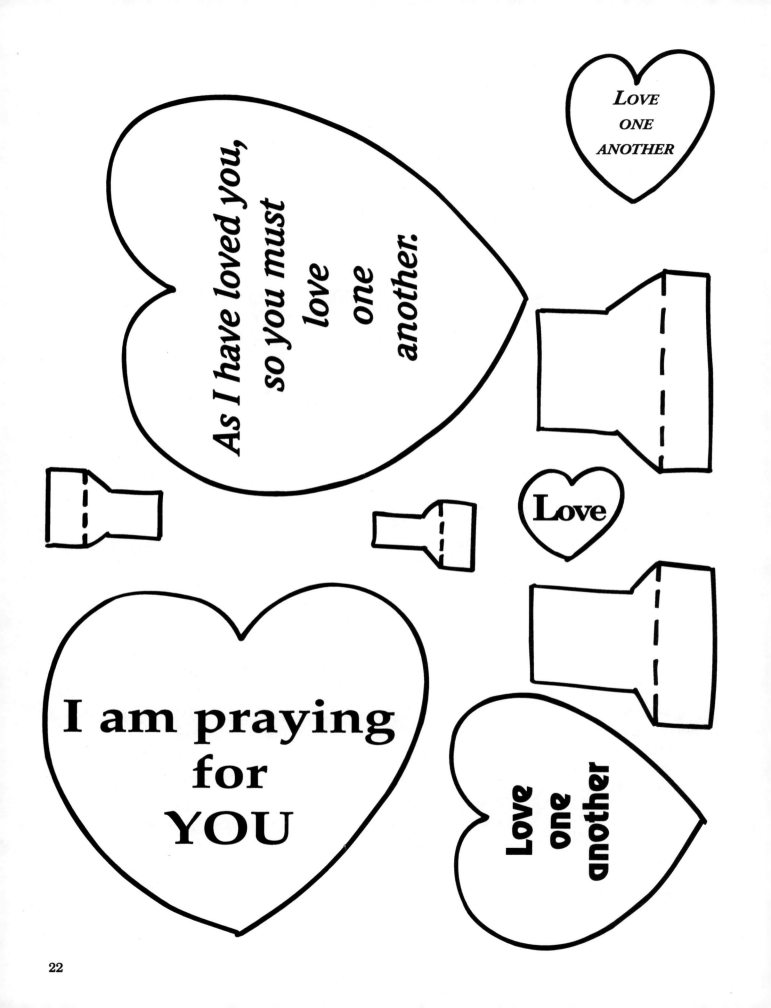

LOVE
ONE
ANOTHER

As I have loved you, so you must love one another.

Love

I am praying for YOU

Love one another

Forgiveness Spinners

 MEMORY VERSE
Forgive as the Lord forgave you. Colossians 3:13

PRAYER THOUGHT
I will forgive others like God forgave me.

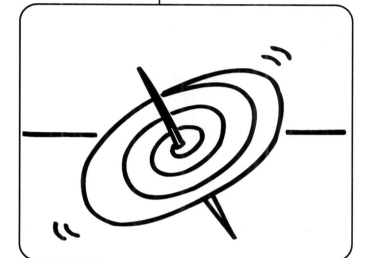

 **ITEMS NEEDED**
page 24, duplicated
crayons or markers
scissors
toothpicks

PREPARATION
Duplicate page 24.

DIRECTIONS

1. Talk about forgiveness as students work. Say, **It is sometimes hard to forgive someone when they hurt us, isn't it? But our memory verse says that we need to forgive others so that God will forgive us. We often forget that we hurt others and need their forgiveness, too.**

2. Assist the students as they color and cut out the circles from page 24.

3. Distribute toothpicks and have them gently poke one through the center of each circle.

4. If time allows, let the students practice spinning their tops.

5. Close with prayer.

Related Lesson
The Parable of the Unmerciful Servant
Matthew 18:21-35

PRAYERS OF COMMITMENT

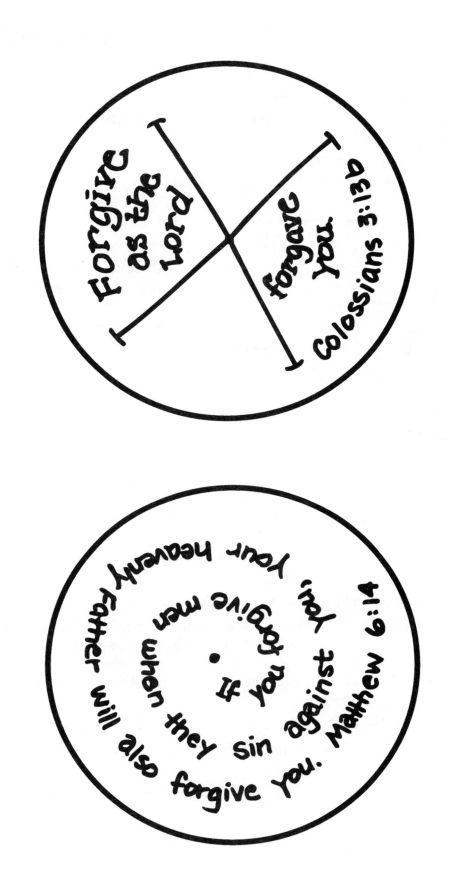

Forgive as the Lord

forgave you.

Colossians 3:13b

If you forgive men when they sin against you, your heavenly Father will also forgive you. Matthew 6:14

Find It Fast Bookmark

PRAYER
Thank You for giving us the Bible from which to read and learn. Amen.

MEMORY VERSE
Put on the full armor of God. Ephesians 6:11

PRAYER THOUGHT
I will learn God's Word.

ITEMS NEEDED
page 26, duplicated
crayons or markers
scissors
tape

PREPARATION

Duplicate page 26. Option: Make two copies of page 26 for each student. They may give the second bookmark as a gift.

DIRECTIONS

1. Help the students to look up each Bible verse on the back of the bookmark (left side when flat) on page 26 using references and discuss why those verses are important. Say, **In some places of the world, people are not allowed to have Bibles or read them. It is important that we take time to learn the Bible and thank God for the instruction and encouragement He gives in His Word.**

2. Assist the students as they cut out the bookmark on solid lines.

3. Show how to fold it at the dashed line and tape.

4. Suggest to the class that they add some favorite Bible verses at the bottom of the back side of the bookmark. Then allow them to color it.

5. If desired, you may give the students two bookmarks to make so they can offer one as a gift to a friend.

6. Close with prayer.

Related Lesson
The Armor of God
Ephesians 6:10-20

PRAYERS OF COMMITMENT

Verses to Remember

Matthew 6:9-13

Matthew 5:3-12

1 Corinthians 13:4-8

Ephesians 6:11-17

John 3:16

Matthew 12:29-31

Ephesians 4:17-32

My Favorite Verses Are...

_____

_____

_____

I will learn Your Word, GOD.

BIBLE

Prayer Calendar

PRAYER
Help me to remember to pray and to give thanks, no matter what happens. Amen.

MEMORY VERSE
Pray continually; give thanks in all circumstances.
1 Thessalonians 5:17-18

PRAYER THOUGHT
I will pray every day.

ITEMS NEEDED
page 28, duplicated
crayons

PREPARATION
Duplicate page 28.

DIRECTIONS

1. Distribute the Prayer Calendars from page 28 and discuss how we can pray for each of the themes represented. Say, **God loves it when we talk to Him.**

2. Encourage the students to use their calendars at home that week by checking off a square each time they pray. They may either color the pictures in class or you can send the sheet with them to color as a take-home project.

3. Review the memory verse with the students.

4. Close with prayer. Afterward, tell the class that they are responsible for remembering to pray on their own the rest of the week (Sunday is not on the calendar because <u>you</u> reminded them to pray today). Suggest that they hang their Prayer Calendar in a place where it will remind them to pray.

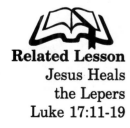

Related Lesson
Jesus Heals
the Lepers
Luke 17:11-19

*PRAYERS OF
COMMITMENT*

28

Candy Bar Car

PRAYER
Dear God, I want
everyone to know
You, so I will tell
others about Your
love. Amen.

MEMORY VERSE
Go into all the world and preach the good news to all creation.
Mark 16:15

PRAYER THOUGHT
I will tell others about God wherever I go.

ITEMS NEEDED
page 30, duplicated
candy bars, 1½" wide maximum
scissors
crayons or markers
tape

PREPARATION

Duplicate page 30. Bring extra candy for snacking.

DIRECTIONS

1. Help the students learn the memory verse as they color and cut out their cars from page 30 on outer solid lines. Say, **What is the Good News that we are supposed to preach? Where do you go?** (school, shopping, restaurants,etc.) **Can you tell people about God in all of those places? How would you do it?**

2. Once the car is cut from the page, assist the class in cutting the car's wheels on the solid lines, using care not to cut the dashed lines.

3. Show how to fold the car upward on the dashed lines. The wheels should bend down to rest on the table.

4. Give each child a candy bar and instruct the class to tape the candy down to the inside of the car. Then show them how to tape the top of the car closed over the candy bar.

5. Close with prayer.

Related Lesson
The Great
Commission
Matthew 28:16-20

*PRAYERS OF
COMMITMENT*

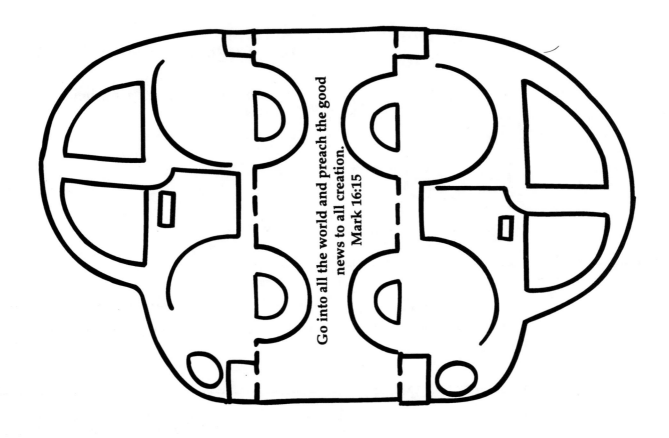

Go into all the world and preach the good news to all creation. Mark 16:15

Courage Clip-it

PRAYER
God, I will turn to You for courage and the strength to be a good Christian. Amen.

 MEMORY VERSE
Christ is faithful...if we hold on to our courage. Hebrews 3:6

PRAYER THOUGHT
I have courage to obey God and follow His ways.

ITEMS NEEDED
page 32, duplicated
clothespins, spring-type
craft sticks
markers
glue
paper

PREPARATION
Duplicate page 32. Construct a model of the finished craft so the students can see what they are making.

DIRECTIONS
1. Discuss the memory verse. Hold up your completed Courage Clip-It and say, **See how this clip holds paper tightly? That is exactly what we need to do with our courage — hold on tightly. Like our memory verse says, God promises to help us hold on to it, even if we are tempted or afraid.**
2. Allow the students to use markers to decorate the clothespins.
3. Help them to glue craft sticks to the ends of the clothespins, as in the illustration on page 32.
4. Distribute page 32 to the students and allow them to cut the verse in the box from the page to clip in the Courage Clip-It. Also pass out plain paper to be clipped.
5. Tell the students the Courage Clip-It can also hold their places in their Bibles or Bible story books.
6. Pray with the class before closing.

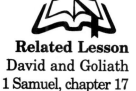
Related Lesson
David and Goliath
1 Samuel, chapter 17

PRAYERS OF COMMITMENT

> *Christ is faithful...if we hold on to our courage.*
>
> Hebrews 3:6

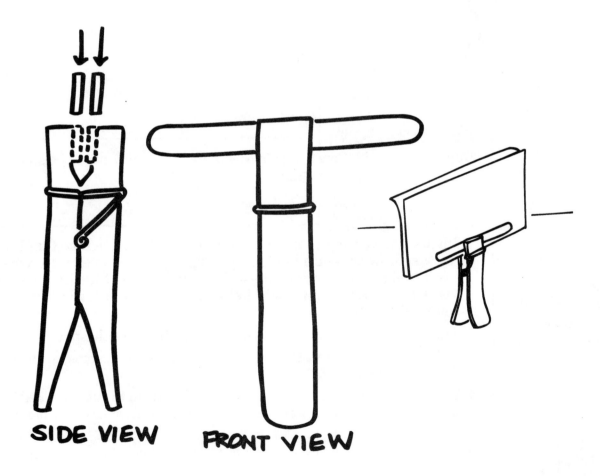

SIDE VIEW   FRONT VIEW

Exercise for the Heart Poster

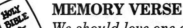 **MEMORY VERSE**
We should love one another. 1 John 3:11

PRAYER THOUGHT
I will exercise my heart by showing love for others.

 **ITEMS NEEDED**
page 34, duplicated
markers

PREPARATION
Duplicate page 34. Write the memory verse on the chalkboard. If your copy machine has enlarging capabilities, consider expanding page 34 to poster-size paper.

DIRECTIONS

1. Help the students to learn the memory verse as they color the poster on page 34. Say, **God wants us to love each other. Just like these children in the pictures are exercising their bodies, we can exercise our hearts. Put your poster on the refrigerator at home to remind you to "exercise your heart" and love one another.**

2. Instruct the students to copy the memory verse to the heart in the center of the page.

3. Close with prayer.

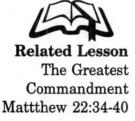
Related Lesson
The Greatest Commandment
Mattthew 22:34-40

PRAYERS OF COMMITMENT

I will exercise my heart by showing love for others.

Prayer Warrior Shield

MEMORY VERSE
For the eyes of the Lord are on the righteous and his ears are attentive to their prayer. 1 Peter 3:12

PRAYER THOUGHT
I can be a prayer warrior.

ITEMS NEEDED
page 36, duplicated
poster board
aluminum foil
paper clips
scissors
glue
markers

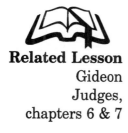

Related Lesson
Gideon
Judges,
chapters 6 & 7

PRAYERS OF COMMITMENT

PREPARATION

Duplicate page 36. You may prefer to cut out one pattern for the larger portion of the shield, trace it onto poster board and cut out one for each child.

DIRECTIONS

1. Assist the children as they cut out the shield from page 36 on the outer solid line. Show them how to trace the shield onto poster board and cut it out.

2. Next, have them cut out the inner shield from the larger paper shield.

3. As the children color the inner shields, talk about prayer. Encourage them to commit to praying every day. Say, **God's eyes are always on us and He is always listening for our prayers. God loves to listen to us. Let's promise Him that we will pray every day. Our Prayer Warrior Shields will remind us of our promise to pray.**

4. Give each child a sheet of foil and show how to cover the larger poster board shields with the foil and secure with tape at the back of the shield.

5. Have them glue the inner shield onto the center of the foil-covered shield.

6. Distribute paper clips and help the children to attach the shields to their clothing.

7. Close with prayer.

Praise Chimes

PRAYER
God, I shout for joy because You are a great God. I worship You with gladness in my heart. Amen.

MEMORY VERSE
Shout for joy to the Lord. Worship the Lord with gladness.
Psalm 100:1-2

PRAYER THOUGHT
I praise God and worship Him with gladness.

ITEMS NEEDED
    page 38, duplicated
    soda cans with pull tabs attached
    wire clothes hangers
    scissors
    tape
    crayons or markers
    string

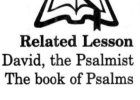

Related Lesson
David, the Psalmist
The book of Psalms

PREPARATION
Duplicate page 38. You will need at least three cans per student. Either provide plain paper for the children to cut out strips and draw their own praise pictures or make extra copies of page 38.

DIRECTIONS
1. Build an atmosphere of praise and worship in the room. Read the memory verse and say, **What does it mean to worship with "gladness"? Does God really want us to "shout" for Him or can we worship in other ways, too?** Let the children name other ways to worship (singing, praying, reading scripture, etc.).
2. As the children color the strips, repeat the memory verse.
3. After they have colored and cut out the strips, show how to tape the strips around the soda cans.
4. Help them hang the cans from the clothes hangers by tying various lengths of string to the tabs on the soda cans, then tie the string onto the hanger.
5. Close with prayer.

PRAYERS OF PRAISE

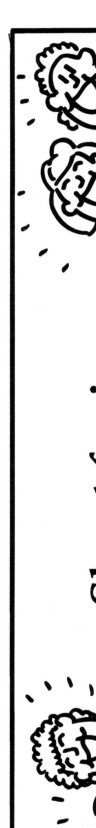

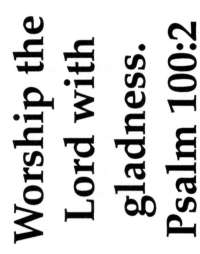

Shout for joy to the Lord. Psalm 100:1

Worship the Lord with gladness. Psalm 100:2

Happy Day Sticker Book

MEMORY VERSE
You have filled my heart with greater joy. Psalm 4:7

PRAYER THOUGHT
Life is better because I know God.

ITEMS NEEDED
> page 42, duplicated
> crayons or markers
> stapler
> tape
> waxed paper
> various stickers
> scissors

PREPARATION

Duplicate page 42. Group several pieces of 10" x 7" waxed paper for each child. Staple the left edge of each stack so the paper will not slide around while students are assembling their books. Cover staples with tape.

DIRECTIONS

1. Stress to the students that God gives us joy in everything. Say, **God is with us no matter what we are doing. This sticker book will remind you that God is with you all of the time — even at play.**

2. Have them cut out the book cover from page 42 on solid lines. Then allow them to color the cover.

3. Help the students to place the waxed paper sheets inside the cover and to staple down the center "binding." Folding the sheets in half first will make this process easier. Pass around tape to cover the staples.

4. Allow the students to select and place stickers in their books. Encourage them to leave space for stickers they may collect later at home or from friends.

5. Repeat the memory verse with the class.

6. Close with prayer.

PRAYERS OF PRAISE

You have filled my heart with greater joy. Psalm 4:7

Soaring Spirit Balloon

PRAYER

Even though I haven't seen You, Lord, I believe in You. You make my spirit soar. Amen.

MEMORY VERSE

Even though you do not see him now, you believe in him and are filled with an inexpressible and glorious joy. 1 Peter 1:8

PRAYER THOUGHT

God makes my spirit soar with joy.

ITEMS NEEDED

page 44, duplicated
plain paper cups, 3 oz. size
scissors
crayons or markers
yarn or string
tape
hole punch

PREPARATION

Duplicate page 44. Gather several hole punch tools for students to share. You will need approximately 18" of yarn or string per student, cut into two longer pieces and one shorter piece.

DIRECTIONS

1. As the students color and cut out the balloons from page 44 on solid lines, help them learn the memory verse. Also, say, **We are filled with such joy because we know Jesus and believe in Him. Doesn't knowing Jesus make you feel like you could soar — just like this balloon?**

2. Have the class fold their balloon together on the dashed line and glue the blank sides together.

3. With a hole punch, show the students how to make holes at the two dots on the bottom of the balloon and one at the top of the balloon.

4. Then help them punch two holes across from one another on the top edge of a cup.

5. Assist them in tying one yarn length from a hole in the bottom of the balloon through a hole in the cup and knot. Repeat with the other hole.

6. Show them how to add a yarn loop through the top hole for hanging.

7. Close with prayer.

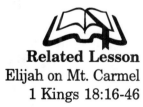

Related Lesson
Elijah on Mt. Carmel
1 Kings 18:16-46

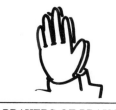

PRAYERS OF PRAISE

43

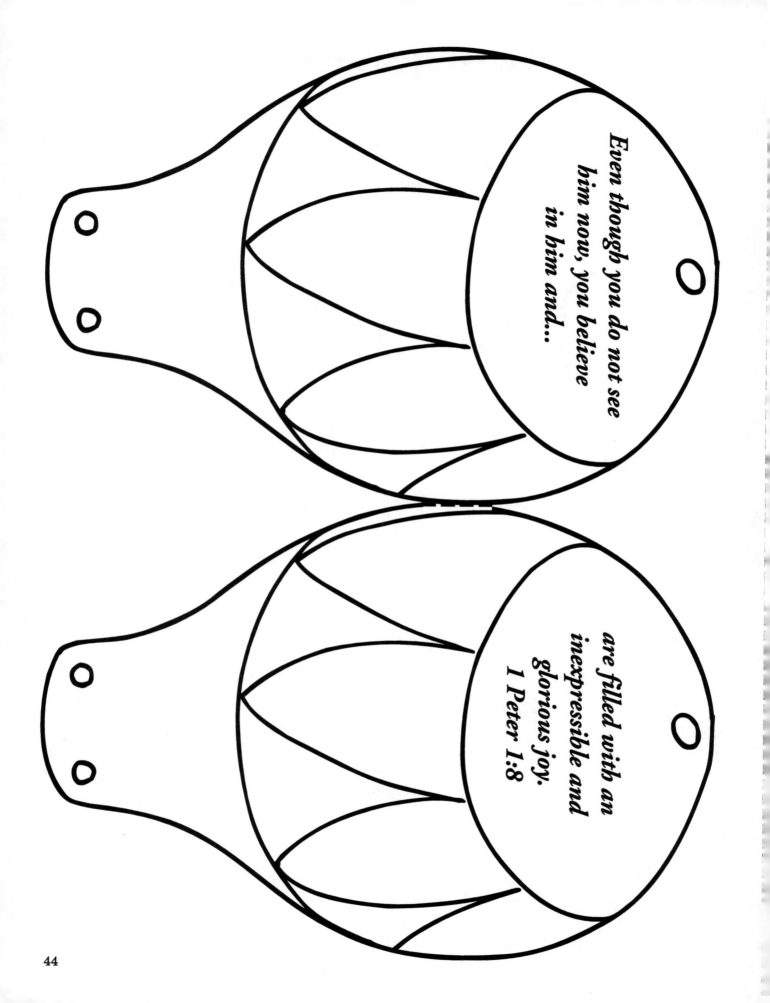

Even though you do not see him now, you believe in him and...

are filled with an inexpressible and glorious joy. 1 Peter 1:8

44

Write-a-Prayer

MEMORY VERSE
Let us go to the house of the Lord. Psalm 122:1

PRAYER THOUGHT
I love to go to God's house and worship Him.

ITEMS NEEDED
page 46, duplicated
pencils
crayons or markers

PREPARATION
Duplicate page 46.

DIRECTIONS

1. Guide the students as they write a prayer on page 46 about the privilege of going into God's house to worship Him. Say, **It is so wonderful to be able to go into the house of our Lord and worship Him! What is your favorite part of worship? Write a prayer on the church and tell God how much you love to worship Him.**

2. Allow the students to color the rest of the picture. Encourage them to take turns reading their prayers aloud while they are coloring.

3. If desired, have the students cut off the edges of the paper and post the prayers on your classroom bulletin board. Or, with the students' permission, talk to your pastor about having the prayers read during worship.

4. Close with prayer.

PRAYERS OF PRAISE

Let us go to the house of the Lord. **Psalm 122:1**

46

Prayer and Praise Pal

PRAYER
You help me to handle any problems that come my way. Thank You for being there to help. Amen.

 MEMORY VERSE
Praise be to the Lord, to God our Savior, who daily bears our burdens. Psalm 68:19

PRAYER THOUGHT
I praise God for always being there for me.

 **ITEMS NEEDED**
page 48, duplicated
chenille stems
crayons or markers
scissors
glue

PREPARATION
Duplicate page 48 for each child.

DIRECTIONS
1. Say, **Have you ever felt alone in your faith? God promises to "bear our burdens," no matter what they are. Today we are going to make a Prayer and Praise Pal. The next time you feel alone, get out your Pal and he will remind you to pray to God for help. Don't forget to praise God when you pray, too.**

2. Guide the children as they color and cut out the pieces to their Pal from page 48 on outer solid lines.

3. Have them fold the Pal's body in half with the illustrated side facing out.

4. Show them how to glue chenille stems on the Pal's body where the arms and legs will attach, inside the fold. Then glue the body together.

5. Show how to fold the hands and the feet over the ends of the chenille stems and glue.

6. Let the students practice bending the Pal into prayer positions.

7. Close with prayer.

Easter Suncatchers

MEMORY VERSE
He has risen! Mark 16:6

PRAYER THOUGHT
I praise God for sending Jesus to save us.

ITEMS NEEDED

page 50, duplicated to transparencies
permanent markers
scissors
string

PREPARATION

Duplicate page 50 to clear transparency sheets (also called "overheads").

DIRECTIONS

1. Have the students cut out the stained glass windows on outer solid lines from the transparencies and color them with markers.

2. Create an atmosphere of praise in the classroom as the students work on their projects. Say, **Isn't it wonderful that Jesus has risen? What a feeling of hope we can have! Our Suncatchers will remind us to always praise God for what He has done for us.**

3. Show how to add a loop of string to the top of each Suncatcher by poking a small hole through the dots on each with the sharp end of scissors (you may want to go around the class and make the holes for the children to prevent possible mishaps with the scissors). Thread string and knot.

4. Close with prayer.

PRAYERS OF PRAISE

Bible Beads

PRAYER
Thank You for telling me about Your love in Your Word. Amen.

MEMORY VERSE
He cares for you. 1 Peter 5:7

PRAYER THOUGHT
I thank God for caring about me.

ITEMS NEEDED
page 54, duplicated
clothespins, spring-type
markers
yarn
scissors

PREPARATION

Make one copy of the example on page 54 and display it in the classroom. Write the memory verse on the chalkboard. You may want to provide extra clothespins so students can make necklaces for friends. For fun, consider making the Friendship Bracelets on page 55 to go with your Bible Beads!

DIRECTIONS

1. Distribute five clothespins per child.

2. Instruct the class to write one word of the memory verse on each clothespin and the Bible reference on the fifth one, holding the clip ends upward. They may also color and draw around the words on the clothespins.

3. As the children work on the necklaces, ask them to share ways in which God takes care of them.

4. To make the neck chain, each child can cut a length of yarn to fit loosely around his or her neck.

5. Show them how to clip the pins over the yarn, keeping the memory verse in the correct order.

6. Close with prayer.

PRAYERS OF THANKS

Friendship Bracelets

PRAYER
You have given me
such good friends.
Thank You for all
of my friends.
Amen

MEMORY VERSE
You are my friends. John 15:14

PRAYER THOUGHT
I am thankful for my friends.

ITEMS NEEDED
page 56, duplicated
crayons or markers
scissors
tape

PREPARATION
Duplicate page 56.

DIRECTIONS
1. Stress to the students that God cares what kind of friends we have. Say, **Isn't it wonderful to have friends? Did you know that God cares who we have as friends? He wants us to have friends that will encourage us to do what is right all of the time. John 15:14 tells us that we are Jesus' friends and He is ours. What better friend could we have than Jesus? He is the perfect example of a friend!**

2. Have the students color the bracelet strips from page 56 and cut them out on the outer solid lines.

3. Help the children to fold the outside edges of the bracelet underneath at the dashed line and tape together.

4. Tell them to keep the bracelet with Jesus' picture for themselves, and to give the other one to a friend. Help them to tape their bracelets on their wrists.

5. Close with prayer.

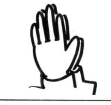

Related Lesson
David and Jonathan
1 Samuel 18:1-4;
19:1-7; 20; 23:15-18

PRAYERS OF THANKS

You are my friends. John 15:14

Thank You, Lord, for my friends.

56

Jesus, My Friend

PRAYER
You are my best friend, Jesus. Thank You for being a friend who stays close. Amen.

MEMORY VERSE
There is a friend who sticks closer than a brother.
Proverbs 18:24

PRAYER THOUGHT
My hand will always be in Jesus' hand.

ITEMS NEEDED
page 58, duplicated crayons or markers

PREPARATION
Duplicate page 58 for each child.

DIRECTIONS

1. Help the children to trace their hand inside the big hand on page 58 with crayons or markers.

2. Say, **Do you have a best friend? Who is it? Did you know we have a Friend who is better than any other friend we could have? It's Jesus! This picture will remind you that Jesus is always available for you. Your hand should always be in His.**

3. Allow them to color the rest of the sheet.

4. Help the class learn the memory verse.

5. Close with prayer.

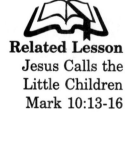
Related Lesson
Jesus Calls the Little Children
Mark 10:13-16

PRAYERS OF THANKS

My hand will always be in Jesus' hand.

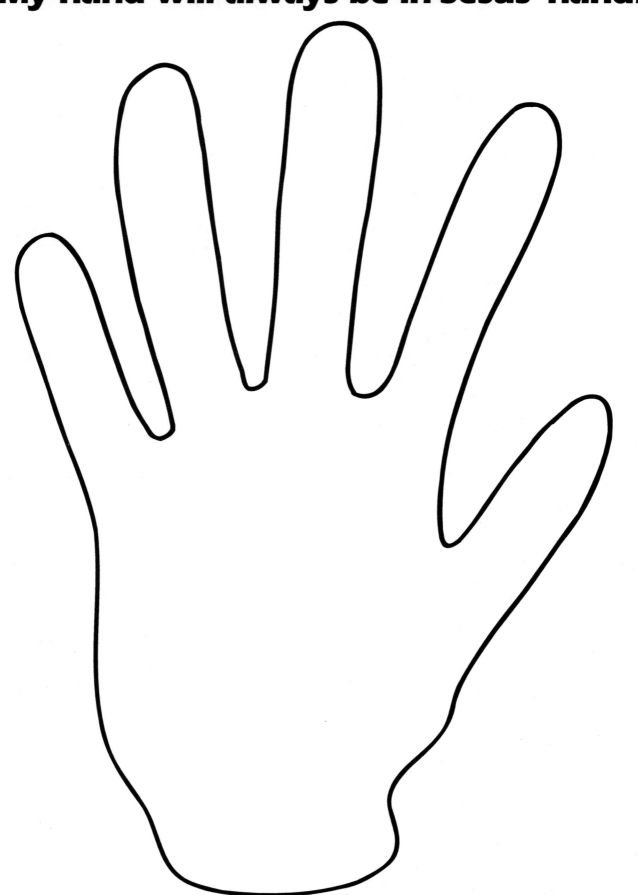

Jesus 'N' Me Switch Covers

PRAYER
Lord, You have
said You will
never leave me.
Thank You.
Amen.

MEMORY VERSE
I will never leave you nor forsake you. Joshua 1:5

PRAYER THOUGHT
I thank the Lord for always being with me.

ITEMS NEEDED

    page 60, duplicated
    crayons or markers
    scissors

PREPARATION
Duplicate page 60.

DIRECTIONS

1. Guide the students as they color and cut out the light switch covers on page 60. Encourage them to make their own designs on the blank version.

2. Explain how the switch cover works (suggest that they check with a parent before taping the cover to a light switch at home). Relate how the cover will remind them that Jesus is the "Light of the World," so we are never alone.

3. Help the class learn the memory verse.

4. Close with prayer.

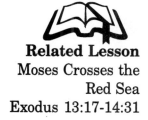

Related Lesson
Moses Crosses the
Red Sea
Exodus 13:17-14:31

PRAYERS OF THANKS

I Am Special

PRAYER
I know You made me for a special purpose. I am fearfully and wonderfully made! Amen.

MEMORY VERSE
I praise you because I am fearfully and wonderfully made.
Psalm 139:14

PRAYER THOUGHT
God made me special.

ITEMS NEEDED
page 62, duplicated
balloons, helium quality
crayons
scissors
glue sticks

PREPARATION
Duplicate page 62. You may want someone to help you inflate the balloons before class. Have extra balloons on hand in case some of them burst.

DIRECTIONS

1. Have the children color and cut out the pieces on page 62 on outer solid lines.

2. Praise the children as they work. Say, **God made each of us special. We are created in His image, but we are each different. This funny balloon character will remind you that each of us is wonderfully made.** Repeat the memory verse.

3. Show how to use a glue stick to secure the features onto a balloon (except for the feet — see step 4). Each child may choose which features to use.

4. Demonstrate how to slice the T on the feet piece (you may want to go around and slice the feet to prevent injury) and push the tied end of the balloon through the T.

5. Remark to the children how unique their balloons are. Then comment on how unique each child is (note differences in hair color, eye color, hair style, etc., but be careful not to draw any hurtful distinctions since children may be sensitive about their appearance).

6. Close with prayer.

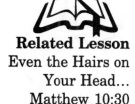
Related Lesson
Even the Hairs on Your Head...
Matthew 10:30

PRAYERS OF THANKS

61

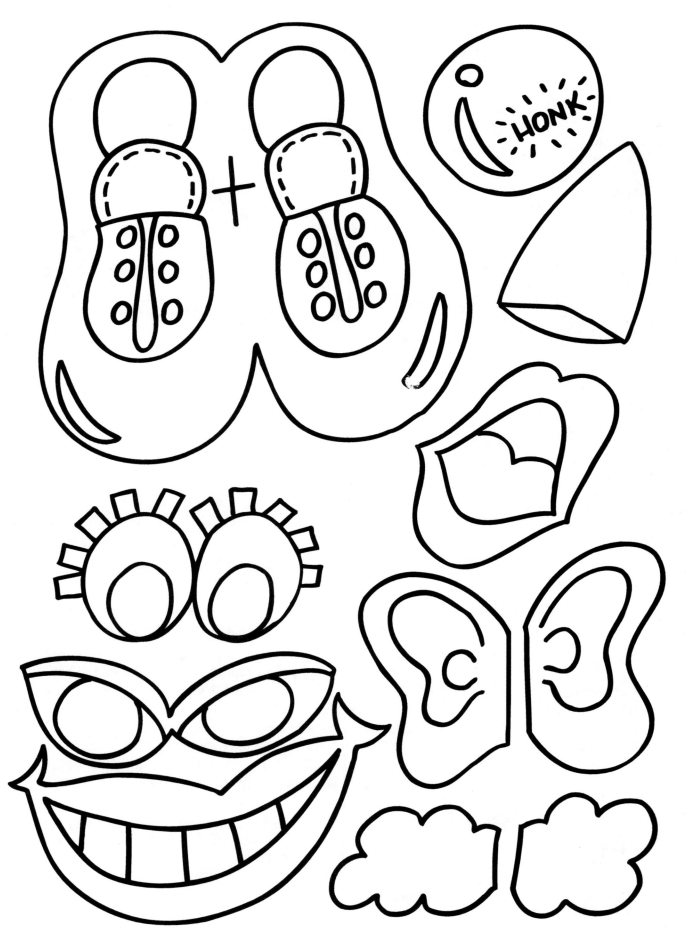

HONK

Plant Pokes

PRAYER
Thank You, God, for Your creation and for allowing me to enjoy it. Amen.

MEMORY VERSE
God..made the world and everything in it. Acts 17:24

PRAYER THOUGHT
God's creation is wonderful.

ITEMS NEEDED
page 64, duplicated
crayons or markers
scissors
glue
craft sticks

PREPARATION

Duplicate page 64. Bring a small, potted plant to show how the Plant Pokes are used.

DIRECTIONS

1. As the children color and cut out the creatures from **page 64** on outer solid lines, have them name some of their favorite creatures in God's world. Remind them to thank God for His wonderful creatures.

2. Help them to fold the figures in half on the dashed line at the top and glue together on the blank side with a craft stick about 1" inside each one.

3. Explain how to use the Plant Pokes at home. Suggest that they check with a parent first before placing a Plant Poke in a pot at home.

4. Pray together before closing.

Related Lesson
Creation
Genesis 1-2:3